Your Organization's Riveting Story:

How to Write So People Will Read, Remember and Respond

Richard Hoefer
Shannon Graves

The Center for Advocacy, Nonprofit and Donor Organizations (CAN-DO)
University of Texas at Arlington School of Social Work
211 S. Cooper Street • PO Box 19129 Arlington, TX 76019

Find us online at www.uta.edu/can-do

Table of Contents

Introduction: About this Report

How a Good Story Turns Readers into Donors

The goal of this report is to help you write an original, expressive, and downright riveting story about your organization. But why? The truth is that stories sell! Advertisers spend billions of dollars on their "brand" - essentially, a story about how their product makes you feel. Lexus inspires luxury and elegance. Apple recalls youth and tech savvy living. Dove Chocolates make us feel like we deserve some decadence.

Consumers and donors have something in common. We all want to invest in things that make us feel good! If you aren't telling a story that elicits powerful feelings about what your organization can do in your community, donors will open their purse strings to someone else who is. There are millions of stories out there, but we'll teach you how to make yours stand out above the rest!

How to Get the Most from This Report

We'd like to suggest a couple of ways to get the most out of this report. While there is no "wrong way" to use it, we've found that it is important to actually work through the steps as you read. If you're working on it by yourself, set aside a short amount of time each day for a week to think carefully about and complete your current step and revise your previous day's work.

At some point, you'll want to show your ideas to others and get their input, but also remember that it is usually easier for others to work from a completed draft than from partially developed ideas. Develop something that you like and can explain, and then make yourself open to feedback.

Another way to use this report is to work on it as a team. Recruit several people from your organization to complete Steps 1 and 2, and then hand off the fine tuning to one person or a designated planning team. Establish a process for approval of the final product.

However you use this report, we hope that it will inspire you to think about your organization's work in a new way! We also hope that if you have any questions about the content here or if find yourself facing challenges that are bigger than the scope of this report, that you will reach out to CAN-DO to have all your questions answered and learn how training and technical assistance from CAN-DO (www.uta.edu/can-do) may be able to help YOU.

Now, let's go through the 7 steps to creating a riveting report that people will read, remember and respond to.

Step 1: Create a Vision

The first step to telling a captivating story is creating a vision that you can actually see and describe in vibrant detail to your audience. Close your eyes. Picture your community as it would be *without* the services of your organization. What do you see? Draw it in the first box below. Don't worry - you don't have to be an artist to be successful! Use cartoons, stick figures, or printed out images from the internet to get your point across.

Here's what your community looks like without you:

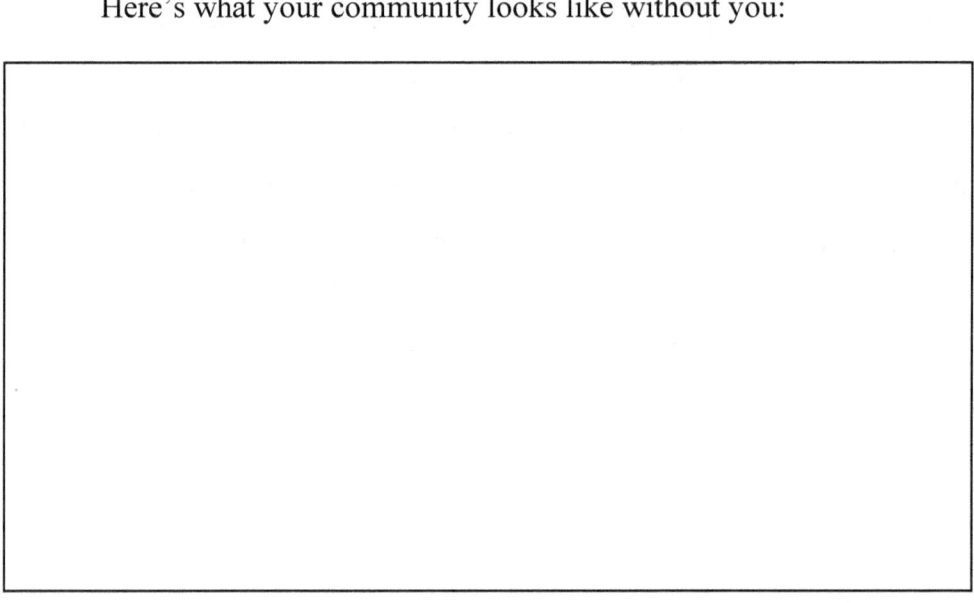

If your vision isn't something you can draw or take a photo of, then look more closely. Is it an individual with a mental illness? A father spending a great deal of time away from his family in order to earn a living? A mother unable to read bedtime stories to her son? If you have a vision that you can't draw, describe on the lines below this paragraph. Use words that evoke emotions in you and your potential audience.

_____

_____

_____

_____

_____

_____

_____

_____

Now, close your eyes again and create a new vision: A vision of a community in which *your organization has totally fulfilled its mission.* What does this community look like? Make a graphic of what your community looks like when your mission is fulfilled:

In the lines below, describe it in detail, with passion! Go ahead... get poetic, romantic. Dream big! Your vision isn't finished yet. Ask others in your organization to complete the same activity and show you what they see. As you mold your vision, remember to keep your target audience in mind. Who are your most likely donors? What "before" and "after" visions are likely to resonate most with their fears and hopes for the community?

_____

_____

_____

_____

_____

_____

_____

_____

_____

_____

_____

_____

_____

_____

_____

_____

A Sample Vision: Community Action for South Texas
From time to time during this report, we'll give you an example from an organization which is not real but demonstrates some common possible solutions to the questions posed here.

Vision of Community without CAST: South Texas' children are hungry, its elderly are isolated, and its workers are idle. An entire way of living is dying as rural communities suffer from infrastructure decay, economic decline, and population out-migration.

Vision Fulfilled with CAST: Rural communities throughout South Texas have the same opportunities as communities throughout the state: Infrastructure needs (including high speed internet and safe roads, highways, and bridges) are met, safe and nutritious food is consumed in proper amounts by all, young and old find common purpose in lifelong learning opportunities and legal methods to earn a living are plentiful.

Step 2: Compile Evidence

Now that you have a "feeling-causing" vision of the conditions your organization is addressing in the community and what fulfillment of your mission is creating, ask yourself an important question:

What evidence do you have
that <u>you</u> are causing your vision to come true?

On the lines below, and off the top of your head, list everything you can think of that helps prove that your organization is already moving the community from Vision A (without you) to Vision B (with you). Write EVERYTHING you can think of down here—this is no time to be modest:

_____

_____

_____

_____

_____

_____

_____

_____

_____

_____

Count Your Widgets

Once you've written everything you can, consider if there's anything you've missed. Even if you don't have a complex evaluation plan in place, you can build an excellent beginning by simply counting your *widgets* - a non-specific word for any "thing" your organization produces (in systems language, these would be called "outputs").

- How many individuals, families, children, or groups have you served this year?
- What about since the inception of your organization?
- How many were people were served by each program you offer?
- How many presentations have you given?
- How many activities or events have you hosted for various purposes?
- How many pamphlets, brochures, or other tidbits of info have you distributed?
- How many partnerships have you formed in the community?
- How many hours were given by your volunteers?
- How many hours were worked by your staff on specific projects and initiatives?

Here are a few more places to dig for information about your widgets and other evidence that shows your organization's value to the community. Circle or highlight the ones that may contribute evidence to the list above with a little digging.

- Past brochures and annual reports
- News articles or stories

- Maps of your service area
- Census or survey data
- Meeting minutes and board reports
- Grant applications and reports

Sample Widgets: Community Action for South Texas
- 50 hours of advocacy to have 2 bridges repaired
- 8,983 pounds of food salvaged/gleaned
- 12 oral history events held for senior citizens
- 67 job training slots filled
- 43 youth returning home

It's important to understand that counting your widgets doesn't actually mean you changed clients' lives, but it does indicate that you are using your funds to get certain things done. For example, CAST indicates it has gathered nearly 9,000 pounds of food, but no one should assume that this means, by itself, that the community has eliminated hunger.

Still, knowing these widgets were produced is a good step on the way to having a riveting story to tell about your organization's accomplishments!

Step 3: Work the Numbers

At this point, you may have a lovely vision and big pile of old reports, numbers, and fragments of ideas about how your organization is working for the good of the community. It's time to make those numbers into something... well, story-worthy! Here are three ways to take your widget numbers and make them memorable!

Add Context to the Numbers

Your numbers alone may not say much by themselves, but by adding context you can create meaning and elicit a stronger emotional reaction from your audience. When sharing a number or statistic, use active language and always emphasize the result rather than the process. Here are a couple of examples:

- Change "103 kids were provided with school supplies" to "We equipped more than 100 students with the tools for academic success."

- Instead of "400 families completed our family services program," try "We reunified 400 families through the use of our evidence-based curriculum."

Adding Context: Community Action for South Texas

Our advocacy to repair the Delgado Bridge saved 50 school children an extra 45 minutes per day by shortening their bus routes, which leaves them more time to study, play and enjoy their childhood. In all we saved over half a million minutes of childhood from being lost on bus rides each year.

We salvaged nearly 9,000 pounds of healthy, locally grown, fresh and nutritious vegetables and fruit - the equivalent of $25,000 in family dollars. That's the cost of preparing 16,000 dinners in a community meal center using government surplus canned food, and our local food is much tastier and better for us.

We produced almost 50 hours of recorded oral history stories during the senior citizen event held each month to connect our past with our future in a way that leads to greater community pride, more appreciation for what our older citizens have endured and a more complete sense of what they have accomplished.

Calculate Costs and Benefits

Another accessible way to add context to numbers is to calculate the costs and benefits of your services and programs. For each initiative that you manage, calculate the total cost of the program and divide it by the total number of beneficiaries served.

Total Beneficiaries / Total Program Cost = Cost Per Client

When you can tell people exactly how much it costs you to create a particular widget or product, you have a very memorable bit of information to share.

Let's apply this simple equation to our previous contextualized statement: "We equipped more than 100 students with the tools for academic success" now becomes *"For less than $20 per student,* we equipped more than 100 students with the tools for academic success." Voila!

> ### *Calculating Costs: Community Action for South Texas*
>
> Think about costs not only in terms of dollars and cents, but also in terms of time and other resources spent and saved.
>
> **Cost in Dollars:** For every $1 spent to salvage or glean local, fresh and nutritious food, we have saved members of our community $5.
>
> **Cost in Hours:** For every hour we spent on advocating for the two bridges to be repaired, we have saved children and working adults nearly 50 hours per year.

Remember: Focus on Change!

As you compile data that supports your organization's effectiveness, remember to keep your eyes on the prize - your vision. Each piece of evidence you uncover should prove that your organization is already working to create the reality of your beautiful vision. While counting widgets is a great start, in the long-term, your organization should develop a comprehensive evaluation plan that measures the outcomes of each strategy and program, not just the numerical outputs. Can we help? CAN-DO! Contact us using the information at the end of this report to learn how you can acquire one-on-one training and technical assistance from highly effective trainers.

Step 4: Take it to the Streets

Numbers are one thing, but in order to create powerful emotions about your organization's effectiveness, you need... well, actual stories! Gather testimonials from clients who have benefitted from your services, volunteers who have connected with their work in a special way, and staff who see the implementation of your vision firsthand every day. Ask them to share with you in their own words how your organization has affected them personally and why they believe in your vision for the community. When appropriate, ask for permission to use their names and possibly even use their photos alongside their testimonials, if they allow you to.

Testimonials: Community Action for South Texas

Before, when the bridge was out, I had to take a long way around to get to my job. I didn't realize just how much time I was losing, it was just part of the daily grind. Now, thanks to the work of CAST, the bridge is fixed. I bet I save an hour a day, easy, and that's time I can play with my kids and help out more around the house.

Erik Hernandez

Testimonials: Community Action for South Texas

Having my grandpa tell his stories used to seem boring. I mean, who wants to hear how it was in the old days? But now that it's on the CAST website in their oral history section, I'm listening to what he has to say, like it was the first time I ever heard him talk. I am so proud of what he's been able to do and so glad his stories are saved.

Donna Jones

Step 5: Get Visual

Speaking of photos, you've certainly heard the phrase "a picture is worth 1,000 words." In telling the story of your organization, this is truer than ever! Think back to those advertisers who are selling you on their product, and more importantly, their brand. Most often, they communicate their brand to you secondarily through words, but first through images. Below are four great ways of many to add touching visual elements to your story.

Take Photos. Take many, many photos of your organization in action. Particularly special are images that capture how your programs and services make people feel. Capture glowing smiles, caring gestures, and human-to-human connections.

Simplify Timelines. Rather than listing a lengthy history of your organization's developments and accomplishments, create a simple timeline that shows the most important stops and commemorates the very special ones with historic images from your past.

Utilize Charts and Graphs. Show trends in community need or organizational outcomes through vibrantly colored and carefully labeled charts and graphs. Consider how you can compare the two side by side and show that increases in your service levels or agency outcomes correspond with decreases in the community conditions you seek to address. When appropriate (think average donor, not government grant application), display revenues and expenses in simple colorful pie charts rather than overly detailed tables.

Create Videos Use the photos you've taken, the timelines you've created, and the charts and graphs you've developed to create a video by using a free editing tool such as Animoto or iMovie. A video feature as short as 30-60 seconds or as long as 3-5 minutes can tell a quick but compelling story of your organization. For more effect, upload to YouTube or other video sharing site.

Step 6: Call to Action

As you piece together the story of your organization, it is vitally important to offer meaningful ways for your target audience to become involved in your work. Don't leave it up to a reader or listener to reach out to you and ask you how they can help. Provide clear, simple, exciting ways to contribute to the work of your organization at different levels of commitment.

Calls to Action: Community Action for South Texas

As CAST works to capture oral histories from the elders of our community, we are in need of up-to-date, gently used video and audio equipment in order to salvage the original detail of recorded accounts. Willing volunteers skilled in editing and managing video files can make a lasting contribution to this project by working with oral histories from home for as little as an hour a week.

Food lovers and amateur (or professional!) chefs can help us to create new traditions by contributing and testing recipes that focus on making healthy meals from fresh local foods. These recipes will be included for generations to come in our community cookbook, which accompanies distributions of our food gleaning program.

What Are Some Ways Your Readers Can Get Involved Now?

Consider how the following readers could contribute to your organization starting today. Be as specific as possible, as if you are expecting a request this afternoon.

- Someone with 1-3 hours per week to give:
- Someone with little time but specialized skill:
- Someone with financial or physical resources:
- Someone who personally knows key decision-makers:
- Other needs (give your own examples):

_____

_____

_____

_____

_____

_____

_____

_____

_____

_____

_____

_____

_____

_____

_____

Step 7: Package Your Story

Think about the best stories you have ever heard and how they were presented to you: a compelling presentation that inspired you, an article or blog entry that motivated you to sign an online petition, or a touching YouTube video that brought you to tears. What makes these stories stand out from the millions that you pass up every day? Most likely, there was something eye (or ear) catching, surprising, exciting, interactive, or heart wrenching about them. These are the same elements that you need to capture in your own story! Consider variations in both storytelling style and presentation format. Be bold in trying on ideas, and pay close attention to how your attempts land with your target audience. Don't be afraid to experiment, but don't be afraid to scrap an idea that isn't working.

Style Your Storytelling

Consider unique ways to frame your story. Tell your story through the voice of a client whose life you have changed (real or imagined). Use familiar metaphors or archetypal storylines to draw the audience in. Portray a client or your organization as a conquering hero. Start with "once upon a time" and end with "happily ever after."

Format Creatively

Even when the words and images of your story are complete, you still have a remaining opportunity to enhance your story through the presentation format. A brochure or handout is useful in formal situations but likely end up in the recycle bin once browsed. Consider presentation options that are reusable or that have a practical function to keep them in sight.

> • Create a video of your story and distribute it electronically.
>
> • Separate your story into 12 key parts and print them on a desk or wall calendar.
>
> • Format your story into a four page spread and print it on a file folder.
>
> • Create a PowerPoint version of your story. Train staff and volunteers to tell it.
>
> • Print your story on the back of your agency letterhead.

Imagination is the only limit here, so be sure to bring several different people into the project at this stage. Each of you will have a different slant to the issues and will have variously differentiated ways of looking at the world. This is wonderful as it provide you with many more ways of coming to see what will make your organization have a riveting story and report.

Wrap-up and Summary

We've presented a 7-step process to help you organize YOUR organization's story, and make it one that your stakeholders will read, remember and *RESPOND* to, with greater involvement and donations.

As a review, here are those seven steps to writing reports that people will read, remember, and respond to.

Step 1: Create a vision.

Step 2: Compile evidence.

Step 3: Work the numbers.

Step 4: Take it to the streets.

Step 5: Get visual.

Step 6: Call to action.

Step 7: Package your story, then share it.

Organizations such as yours need to be engaging and this report provides you with empirically supported ways to garner additional interest in your work, by helping YOU focus on ways to be "riveting"—yielding more connections between your organization and the people you want to connect with.

If you've found the information in this report useful, be sure to look carefully at the next pages to find out more about CAN-DO and what some of CAN-DO's other information products are.

Can We Do Something More for You?

CAN-DO! To learn more about how to develop attention-getting short reports, videos, training, and other technical assistance, contact Dr. Rick Hoefer at rhoefer@uta.edu. Dr. Hoefer is the Roy E. Dulak Professor for Community Practice Research in the School of Social Work at the University of Texas at Arlington. He directs the Center for Advocacy Nonprofit and Donor Organizations (CAN-DO).

Dr. Hoefer specializes in translating cutting edge, best practice research into usable practice points for organizations. His passion is helping nonprofits succeed in providing high quality services to our communities. He has over 25 years of experience working in and with nonprofit organizations, assisting them in improving their services through program evaluation, advocacy, and management consulting. Dr. Hoefer has authored more than 30 published journal articles and 6 books and has given scores of presentations in the field of nonprofit management, advocacy and policy practice.

Shannon Graves is a consultant with experience in nonprofit management, fund development, strategic planning, and community organizing. She specializes in bringing best practices to service systems and organizations through the effective and innovative development of policies, programs, and people.

Learn More with Video Resources by CAN-DO

For timely CAN-DO tips and resources, subscribe to Dr. Hoefer's YouTube channel by searching for DrRickHoefer. You may also visit www.uta.edu/can-do for links to these highly ranked videos:

3 Ways to Raise More Funds Online:
https://www.youtube.com/watch?v=uwOBHV8JwLc

Decision-making Flow Chart:
https://www.youtube.com/watch?v=8ptq1SR0wok

Five Steps on How to Hire an Evaluator:
https://www.youtube.com/watch?v=hMEEBZJT4uE

How to Decrease Staff Turnover:
https://www.youtube.com/watch?v=GQqhsNsfWmc

How to Handle Nonprofit Mission Drift:
https://www.youtube.com/watch?v=m5Kwa8UnRIY

How to Use Grants.gov to Find Federal Grants:
https://www.youtube.com/watch?v=yDbGerr5Oek

Leadership and Learning Organizations:
https://www.youtube.com/watch?v=fdojiqAb9Ss

The Ethics of Advocacy:
https://www.youtube.com/watch?v=4x5PnVrt5zw

What Can CAN-DO Do for You?
https://www.youtube.com/watch?v=c8YR8ivyBPo